Correspondence With God

The Heart of Prayer Captured In Letters To Our Lord

Nancy Tuttle

ACKNOWLEDGMENTS

My heartfelt thanks go out to all those who loved and supported my mom, including the members of St. Andrews Church, her Spiritual Wellness Group, and her longstanding Minion Covenant group. My sincere gratitude also goes out to those at Saddleback Church and All About GOD Ministries, including Bob, Greg, Candy, Peg, Jennifer, Ray and Nadre, who shared in the words and tears of this project. I love you all!

My heart and soul go out to my precious wife, Debra, who gave me the time and understanding to pursue this project in Mom's memory. This work is also dedicated to my stepfather and Mom's dear husband, Bob, who endured side-by-side with Mom until the very end. I am absolutely blessed to have such a loving and supportive family.

In Christ,

Randall Niles

Cover design by Nadre Davani, based on
Jan van Eyck's "St. Barbara" (c.1437),
Koninklijk Museum voor Schone Kunsten, Antwerp.

ISBN: 0-9678230-6-4

Requests for information should be addressed to:
Kenosis Publishing, LLC.
20532 El Toro Road
Suite 209
Mission Viejo, CA 92692
www.KenosisPublishing.com

Printed in the United States of America.
Published October 2002.

PROLOGUE

After seven years of battling breast cancer, my mother, Nancy, went home to be with the Lord. She was a phenomenal witness and testament for what "true Christianity" is all about. Mom was humble, loving, and gave tirelessly of herself for God. She was also strong, uncompromising and determined to make a difference in the lives of those God brought to her. Over 250 people celebrated her life at her memorial service. It was dramatic to see the impact she had on so many people in so many positive ways. Everyone agreed she had fought the good fight, finished the race, and kept the faith!

One of the last messages Mom received from God was "to write." Although she never fully understood God's purpose for this calling, she accepted the challenge with a servant's heart. As my mother's health declined, she was increasingly frustrated with her lack of mental focus and discouraged that her lack of physical strength prevented her from accomplishing God's work.

About one month after her death, God revealed to me that His calling for my mother was not yet complete. Through a series of visits and letters from Christian friends who knew and loved her, God hit my heart with the fact that I was part of this "calling!" As a prodigal son, I was integral to God's purpose for Mom's life!

Filled with conviction, I returned to her desk, computer, files and bookshelves in order to discover the full impact of God's calling. I was stunned to find a wealth of material she had been inspired to write over the years. Letters, journals, testimonies, essays, church devotionals, Bible study notes – they were fantastic, rich with insight and heart. She covered topics such as Christianity, marriage, motherhood, relationships, trials, victories, and life purpose.

In tears, I collected my mother's works and spent that weekend reading. In prayer, I humbly realized that I was a prodigal son saved by God's patient grace. Through my mother's words, I saw that my relationship with Jesus was the ultimate hope and purpose for her life of fervent prayer.

Immediately after this weekend experience, God put people and circumstances in my life that made my newfound assignment dramatically clear:

I was to fulfill my prodigal legacy by organizing Mom's various writings and sharing them with the world...a world that desperately needs to know about God's patience and love!

By God's grace, this is the second in a series of books I feel called to share. Through letters to God, my Mom poured out her heart as a Christian woman. I hope you enjoy her thoughts, prayers, dreams, heartaches and insights. I hope you are touched in some wonderful way.

And I, brethren,when I came to you, came not with excellency of speech or of wisdom, declaring unto you the testimony of God. For I determined not to know any thing among you, save Jesus Christ, and him crucified. And I was with you in weakness, and in fear, and in much trembling. And my speech and my preaching was not with enticing words of man's wisdom, but in demonstration of the Spirit and of power: That your faith should not stand in the wisdom of men, but in the power of God.

I Corinthians 2:1-5 KJV

PART ONE

"BE NOT DISMAYED"

After two failed marriages, I hit a low point in my life. Within a month, my second husband left, our house was sold and my beloved only child, Randy, went across the country to attend Georgetown University. As a teacher, I transferred to a new school and grade level where I knew no one, I moved into an apartment that didn't allow pets, and I had to give my silky terrier to my mother. My new apartment number was 9-1-1 and I needed all the help I could get! The trees surrounding my lower level apartment resembled a cave into which I retreated at the end of each day. I prayed that God would show me His will and teach me to obey. I spent hours writing letters to God in my journal and, sometimes, even writing the answers that He revealed to me as I meditated.

Letter to God

Dear Heavenly Father,

I need Your solace and peace in this difficult situation. I feel so worthless and ineffectual, yet I feel a wisdom, and a patience, and a lack of self-pride, which must come from You, as I can't claim it as mine. I wish I could see Your plan for our lives. Everything looks so hopeless now. Please guide me. What do I need to do?

You and Your world are so great, and I am so small – who am I that You care, but You do. I feel Your care, and I'm so thankful. I know You have a wonderful plan for my life. Please open it one day and one step at a time – and keep me from getting in the way.

Thank You for Your word today about King Solomon asking for wisdom. Help me to see how I should ask so that I may improve during this crisis and not fall victim to the world and my worldly desires. Be with Randy and help me explain things to him. Keep him in Your paths. Give me wisdom to continue guiding him in Your way. Thank You for Your hand on him thus far. Thank You for letting me have him for a while.

Love,

Nancy *April 1984*

Letter from God

Dear Nancy,

Wait on Me and My timing.

It's OK to improve yourself.

Don't be afraid to be alone. I'll be with you.

I love you!

August 1984

Fear not, for I am with you.
Be not dismayed; for I am your God.
I will strengthen you; Yes, I will
help you; I will uphold you
with My righteous right hand.

Isaiah 41:10 NKJV

I have refined you, but not as silver;
I have tested you in the furnace of
affliction. I am the Lord your God,
who teaches you to profit, Who leads
you by the way that you should go.

Isaiah 48:10,17 NKJV

Letter to God

Dear God,

This is the beginning of the second half of my life – the beginning of a new life. Please be with me and guide me. Help me to learn from the past. Give me a wisdom I have lacked, a love for others (without so much concern for myself), an optimism and enthusiasm for the future, and a closeness to You.

Thank You for all You have given me – family and friends who love me, a beautiful son, a good job, enough money, health, looks, enough brains, an okay personality, and my faith in You.

I would like to think I am a clean slate that I can dedicate to You to use as You wish, but in reality, I am me – a total of my past experiences and a special person created by You. So You're going to have to meet me where I am, and use me as I am, because that's ME and I guess You knew what You were doing when You made me.

I need a home where I can be happy and where I can grow this year. I need a church where I can grow, pray, study Your word, have a support group, some social life, and find joy and understanding. I need friends. I need to get financially stabilized. I want to get my life organized and grow spiritually and relationally.

Thank You for being there. Be with everyone I love. Thank You for loving me so I can love myself – and others – and You.

Love,
Nancy

August 1984

Letter to God

Hi God,

It's been a while since I've taken time to write You a note. Thanks for being there whenever I call and not being too busy to listen. How do You do it? How can I learn to do it?

I praise You for Your loving care. Thank You for protecting Randy and me. Please continue to do so. Lead me in Your ways. Give me discernment to know what is Your way and what is not.

Please keep me in Your paths. I love You and I need Your love.

I need You in my life. I mess things up in my own wisdom. Thank You for caring and for providing. Thanks for friends.

It was wonderful having family over the holidays. I have a better feeling of who I am, although it also intensifies the loneliness now that they're gone. Thank You Lord for hope and joy in the future. Help me to be patient and to trust in Your timing.

I Love You,
Nancy — *January 1985*

Letter from God

Nancy, be patient.
I have a wonderful plan for
you, but there is much to do
to ready you, and lots of
healing that needs to take place.
I love you dearly.

February 1985

Letter from God

Nancy,

I love you. I shed My own blood for you to make you clean. You are new, so believe it is true. You are lovely in My eyes, and I created you to be just as you are. Do not criticize yourself or get down for not being perfect in your own eyes. This leads only to frustration. I want you to trust Me, Nancy, and take one day at a time. Dwell in My power and love and be free. Be yourself. Don't allow other people to run you.

I will guide you if you will let Me. Be aware of My presence in everything. I give you patience, love, joy, and peace. Look to Me for answers. I am your Shepherd and will lead you. Follow Me only. Do not ever forget this. Listen and I will tell you My will. I love you, Nancy. I love you! Let it flow from you, spilling over to all you touch.

Be not concerned with yourself; you are My responsibility. I will change you without you hardly knowing it. You are to love yourself and to love others simply because I love you. Take your eyes off yourself; look only to and at Me. I lead, I change, I make, but not when you're trying; I won't fight your efforts.

You are Mine, Nancy. Let Me have the joy of making you like Me. Let Me give you joy, peace, and kindness. No one else can. You're not your own. You have been bought with blood and now belong to Me. Your only demand is to look to Me and only Me, never to others. Don't struggle. Relax in My love. Stop trying. Let Me make you what I want. My will is perfect, My love sufficient. Look to Me.

I love you Nancy.

February 1985

Letter from God

Dearly Beloved,

I beseech you as a pilgrim to abstain from fleshly lusts which war against the soul. If you want to do great things for the Kingdom, begin by obeying Me in the small things. I love you.

February 1987

Note to God

Dear Lord,

Thank You for Your strength and encouragement!
I say, "yes" to the future!
I am tired of feeling stressed about things
I have no control over.
I can make positive decisions about
how to live each day.
I can turn to You and other Christians
for guidance and strength.
I can plan for the future so I always have
things to look forward to.
I can love myself and take good care of
myself, while loving others at the same time.
I will not let myself get pulled down
emotionally by the depression of others.
I will take time to strengthen myself
in You so I can reach out to others.
I will face the future with hope.
To all that shall be – Yes!
Thank You Lord for Your blessings.
Help me be the best that I can be.

Love,
Nancy

October 1988

Notes from God

Nancy,

Get wisdom.

Keep the commandments.

Have pity on the poor and give to them.

Seek counsel of Christians.

Fear the Lord.

Cease listening to worldly knowledge.

Nancy,

Read the Bible daily.

Pray on your knees daily.

Wake up on time.

Drink water, not alcohol.

Eat fruit, vegetables and grains.

Exercise.

Reach out to others.

October 1988

Letter to God

On the eve of my 49th birthday…

God,

Only You can count the number of my days, but I feel I have 15 productive years left. Give me a vision for those years. Use me for Your glory. I have read through Your Word this past year and am condemned by my lack of obedience and my waste of time and energy. Take away my uncertainties and fears. Give me positive direction. Help me be positive with others. Help me be content where You have put me, and use my discontent to help me grow into the person You would have me be.

You are so gracious unto me. You know my inward parts, thoughts, and struggles. You love me and have an excellent plan for me. Give me Your peace. Help me to walk in Your ways. I can't do it on my own.

Fill me with Your love.

Amen,
Nancy

February 20, 1990

Letter to God

Dear God,

I'm tired of illness, depression and old things. I crave lightness, hope, health and future. Help me to get rejuvenated and to pass my energy on to those about me.

Love,
Nancy

July 1993

Response from God

Sweet Nancy,

Go thy way;
thy faith has made thee well!

Write...

July 1993

Letter to God

Dear Lord,

Thank You for calling me to
write about my life.

Thank You for the life You
have given me.

Your Daughter,
Nancy

Show me thy ways, O Lord;
Teach me thy paths.
Lead me in thy truth
and teach me;
For thou art the God
of my salvation;
On thee do I wait all the day.

Psalm 25:4-5 KJV

July 1993

The Lord is my rock, and my fortress, and my deliverer;
My God, my strength, in whom I will trust;
My shield, and the horn of my salvation, my stronghold.

Psalm 18:2 NKJV

As for God, His way is perfect;
The word of the Lord is proven;
He is a shield to all who trust in Him.

Psalm 18:30 NKJV

PART TWO

"FINISHING THE RACE"

In 1994, my son fell in love with Debra and married her. I had been praying for his wife for years, and Debra matched my every hope. I too, found my true love at this time. I married Bob two months before Randy and Debra's wedding. I was so happy. I had a loving husband, an apartment with a view of the ocean, my son and his darling wife living nearby, and an active life between teaching a fifth grade gifted class, church activities such as leading a Stephen Ministry class, and daily walking, swimming or biking with Bob.

Six months later, I was diagnosed with breast cancer. After a mastectomy, breast reconstruction, and daily hormone medication to prevent a recurrence, I treated my cancer as just a bump in the road of life. However, when the breast cancer metastasized to my spine in 1997, I knew my days were numbered. Only God knows the number and His timing is perfect. So I put my trust in Him and He gave me these last years to see His wonderful plan being worked out in the lives of those I love. I have had eight different types of chemotherapy, three types of hormone treatments, and two rounds of radiation – and I have been absolutely blessed.

I have been blessed to see all three of my grand-babies come into this world and to get to know each of them as unique individuals created by God. I wish I could be around as they grow to celebrate their successes and special occasions with them, but I am comforted and assured to know they are being raised in a Christian home.

The greatest blessing of all has been to witness Randy's return to a believing faith in Jesus Christ after twenty years of questioning, agnosticism, and even atheism. As a believing mother, my fervent prayer over the years was that my son would become a "great man of God." Who knows how God works? But His Holy Spirit is like a choreographer, "working everything for good for those who love Him and have been called according to His purpose."

Meditation With God

Who Am I?

I'm a Christian who has lost my savor.
I'm task-oriented, not people-oriented.
I'm self-sufficient and independent.
I'm a teacher.
I serve God and get weary.
I'm a wife, mother, grandmother,
sister, daughter, niece and friend.

Lord, What do You See in Me?

My child, I see a precious person who tries so hard to keep everything under her control that she is missing much of the joy and freedom I have for her. Relax, let Me do it, enjoy, learn new things – grow. I have a wonderful plan for your life and Bob's.

Where Do I Need to Change?

I need to become more spicy!
Lord, give me a tender heart.
I need to let go and let God, and be open
to experiencing His surprises and joy.
Open me, Lord, to being a learner and to
allowing the Holy Spirit to work through me.
Help me to touch others with Your love.

September 1994

Message from God

Praise Me through trial.

See My bigger picture.

Find quiet times with Me.

Find peace by trusting Me.

Be open to My Holy Spirit to reach others for Me.

Reflection on God's Message

God will triumph.

God gives us what we have.

God is all-powerful.

Who can question God?

God is so much greater than we are.

God works wonders.

God is the great Creator
(everything of man's is vanity).

Glory to God, Who keeps me from falling.

1997

Conversation With God

Dear God,

It's the beginning of a new year. What will 1998 hold for me?

Pain and blessings, life and death, spiritual growth unbounded, love of others and for others, strength to endure, courage to face trials, enthusiasm about the future, and a renewed faith.

God, thank You for being with me through chemotherapy. Thank You for the blessings that are coming as a result.

Anyone who seeks God with all his heart and all his soul will find Him.

The word of God is very near – in my mouth and in my heart when I study the Bible.

If Christians humble themselves, pray, seek God's face, and turn from their wicked ways, God will hear, forgive their sins, and heal their land. God listens!

Blessed is the person God chooses to approach Him. If you believe in your heart and confess with your mouth, you will be saved.

We have bold access with confidence by faith in Jesus Christ. Jesus can feel our infirmities because He was a man, so we can boldly come to the throne and find mercy and grace to help in times of need.

Thou wilt keep her in perfect peace, whose mind is stayed on Thee, because she trusts in Thee. Trust in the Lord forever; for in God is everlasting strength.

What do You want me to do with the rest of my life?

Wait on the Lord. Be of good courage, and I will strengthen your heart.

Mount up with wings like eagles, run and not be weary, walk and not faint.

Learn to number your days, that you may apply your heart unto wisdom.

God makes everything beautiful in its time.

Thank You for being there, for caring, and for Your mercy and grace.

Love,
Nancy

January 1998

Letter to God

Dear God,

Give me the strength to face further cancer treatments. Help me see ways to use this painful time to pray with feeling for others.

Thank You for Randy. Through my love for him, I know how much You love me.

Nancy *February 1998*

Letter to God

Dear God,

I've been busy in the process of retiring from 33 years of teaching and searching for alternative cures for my cancer. I know that my faith in Your healing power is my best alternative. I'm sorry my priorities have focused on other methods of healing. Please guide me, give me Your peace, and help me reach out to others with Your love and peace. I am thankful that You opened the doors to my retirement.

Forgive me, Lord, for leaving my first love — You. I've been taking You for granted, knowing You are always there for me. I guess I'm confused and angry about my battle with cancer. Do not forsake me. I need You beside me to hold me up when I stumble.

I Love You,
Nancy

August 1998

Letter to God

I awoke early on the morning after my 58th birthday with a craving to write to You, God. But I couldn't find my new journal and in the dark I grabbed this old one and found precious promises and guidance You've given me over the years.

A year ago, I feared I might not make it to this birthday and here I am – and feeling "good." My oncologist even said I was "doing good" this month after over a year of chemotherapy and radiation. He credited chemo, prayer and our cruise to Hawaii. I also think love has a lot to do with my healing.

What a wonderful birthday weekend. I had wanted to get away, but everything I love most was right here. Bob and I had a romantic dinner on the water on the eve of my 58th. Then church with Bob in the choir singing, "One Faith, One Hope, One Love," and so much to be thankful for, especially Randy's attending church and talking to You. And finally, all the joys and hugs of a birthday dinner with the grandbabies. So many blessings…

Thank You for caring for my aunt Jo and bringing her to You in her end times – once I let go, and let You. Thank You for my sister's love and that of her family. I don't understand what You are doing in Mom's life, but I know You love her and that You have a plan. Please be very close to her. Thank You for my family's love.

This quiet time with You is precious. It is a gift that is always available if I will seek it. Help me to open myself to You and Your love – to do Your will with the days You have ordained for me to live upon this earth until I go home to be with You.

With Love,
Nancy

February 1999

Letter to God

Dear God,

Thank You for my cancer – You are in control and You do love me. You know what is best for me and my loved ones. You have a plan. Help me to trust in You and be part of Your plan.

Thank You, God, for loving us enough to send Your precious Son, Jesus Christ, to live, to teach us about You, and to die in order to give us forgiveness for our sins.

Thank You for the opportunity to be a mother (and the awesome responsibility that is). Thank You for being there in the midst of my many shortcomings. Use my cancer to help me teach Randy about You and to be a godly influence in the lives of my stepchildren and grandkids and husband and aunt and mom and sister and her family and friends and everyone I meet.

Thank You for using cancer as a teacher for me – to slow me down and put me in touch with You. Help me see cancer as a teacher and an adventure to learn from and then go on. Bless Bob and Randy and my supportive family and friends as they go through this adventure with me. Make us strong through our weakness and our dependence on You.

Thank You for Your <u>many</u> blessings. They are too numerous to count. Help me to bury the ghosts of sins past, which You have forgiven and forgotten. And help me to see and confess my daily sins, so I can better mirror Christ's love and be used more mightily by You.

Love,
Nancy

December 1999

Letter to God

Dear God,

I am writing this letter to tell You how much I love You. I love You because You first loved me. You loved me so much that You sent Your son to earth to light my way and to show me how to be Your child through faith in Jesus Christ, Your son. Thank You for choosing me – for Your mercy and grace to adopt me as Your daughter. Thank You for opening my eyes and softening my heart to accept Your truth and Your love.

I can never thankou enough for justifying me through the blood of Your Son, so that I may talk freely with You as my daddy and someday stand before You as perfectly forgiven and cleansed from my sinful nature and disobedience. You are so holy and righteous and awesome that there is no other way I could dare to come and kneel before Your throne. There is nothing I could do to deserve this honor. It is only by Your grace that I can come into the light of Your presence.

I am what I am, and yet You love me. Thank You for creating me and for giving me my Christian parents, who taught me from age nine Your ways. Thank You for Your abounding grace, which is all-sufficient to help me know Your plan for my life and to be obedient to do Your will.

Lord, forgive me when I go my own way and do not seek Your path. Forgive me when I am proud of my own works and do not give You the credit. Thank You for humbling me so I can see You working in my life. I am sorry for the times I seek the praise of others, rather than honoring You.

Thank You for giving me Your wisdom when I ask. Help me not to be like a wave of the sea, driven with the wind and tossed by the problems of this world. Help me not to be double-minded, but to follow in Your ways, rather than in the ways of the world.

Thank You for using me and my story to reach out to others with Your love and Your Gospel. Fill me with Your Holy Spirit on Monday so I may speak Your words, not my own. Bring that one person to my talk for Christian Outreach Week whose heart You want touched, and use me to touch her.

You are a loving, merciful and awesome God, and I love You.

In Your Grace,
Nancy

March 2000

Letter to God

God,

Cancer has made me aware that my time on earth is temporary. I don't want to waste my days with meaningless activities. I want to choose to spend my time doing things that will help me to grow more Christ-like. God, I give You my time.

Your Child,
Nancy

January 2001

Letter to God

Lord,

Today was my 60th birthday! I can't believe I'm 60!! I don't feel old. But I feel blessed by You to be alive. I know my days are numbered and that You are the only one who knows how many days I have left here on earth. I am so thankful that You have chosen to let me live this long so I can get to know my grandchildren, see my son and daughter-in-law grow in their love of You, finish my memoirs, and minister to others with cancer. I am also thankful that You have allowed me to be here for Bob, rather than adding another lost loved one to his tragedies.

Love,
Nancy

February 2001

Message from God

Nancy,

Your life is a vapor that appears for a little time and then vanishes away.

Don't become enamored of your plans for tomorrow. Remember, your time is in My hands and each day is a gift from Me. One day, I will call you to be with Me, so make the most of today, keeping eternity in mind.

July 2001

Message to God

Lord,

I thank You for allowing me the time to be a spiritual matriarch for our family. Even though I hardly see myself as an example of the Christian life, I'm glad others see Christ in me through the indwelling of the Holy Spirit. I live to finish my spiritual race with joy, and to complete Your task for me of bringing my loved ones to You.

July 2001

God's Whisper

I was awakened at 4:30 a.m. by a voice whispering my name, "Nancy." The Lord was gently waking me from a deep sleep by speaking my name inside my head. Although God has awakened me in the middle of the night on several occasions and I have been led to pray for specific things that later proved to need prayer, I had not heard Him speak my name before. I fell to my knees beside my bed. I did not need to take off my shoes in this holy place, because my feet were already bare.

"Nancy, I am going to bless you. I am going to bless you out of your socks! Let Me and I will speak through you." I felt honored and humbled that God would choose to speak through me. I pray that I will be open to His leading and His words through the Holy Spirit. I feel that I need to get on more intimate terms with Him.

Dear Lord, I feel confident that You will do what You have promised. I am on borrowed time and am thankful that You have allowed me to live with cancer and the treatments for seven years. I thank You for everything! How do You wish to use me? Perhaps You will speak through me to my new core group at Community Bible Study, or through the book, "Prayers for a Prodigal", that my son and I are looking to write together, or when I tell my story to the choir in two weeks...

My mind is in high gear, but I am no longer listening to the Lord.

I should have stayed on my knees asking God who needed prayer instead of writing in my journal and retreating to my cozy bed and sleep. I missed a blessing God had for me. At 7:00 a.m., my son called to tell us to turn on CNN. He said, "We are at war! The World Trade Center and the Pentagon have been bombed!"

Bob and I sat in disbelief as we watched the horror repeated over and over on TV as hijacked airliners full of passengers crashed into the towers of the World Trade Center. Then the towers, full of people, fell one by one, and smoke billowed into the sky over Manhattan. A third plane crashed into the Pentagon causing a huge gash and again killing many Americans. A fourth plane, with Camp David or the White House as its target, crashed outside Pittsburgh killing all aboard.

I was speechless. I dressed to go to my training meeting to be a leader at Community Bible Study. Bob held my hands and said a beautiful prayer for our country, our president, the injured and the families of all those who had died, as well as for the perpetrators of this horror. I could not pray. I went to the training meeting where we spent the first hour on our knees praying, but again I could not speak. I am in shock most of the day and find it hard to say or pray anything meaningful. I just listen as those around me weep and pray eloquently.

I pray that God will give me words tomorrow for the fifteen women He has chosen to be in my core group and that, together, we will heal from this tragedy. I pray that this tragic day will unite our country as never before and that we will return to the faith that has made our country strong.

September 11, 2001

Joyous Verses from God

The joy of the Lord is (my) strength.

Nehemiah 8:10 NIV

Count it pure joy, my brothers whenever you face trials of many kinds, because you know that the testing of your faith develops perseverance. Perseverance must finish its work so that you may be mature and complete, not lacking anything.

James 1:2-4 NIV

However, I consider my life worth nothing to me, if only I may finish the race (with joy) and complete the task the Lord Jesus has given me.

Acts 20:24 NIV

January 2002

Letter to God

God,

*I will find **joy** in each day,*
praise Your name, and
speak to others about
Your love and grace!

January 2002

The Lord is my rock,
my fortress, and my savior;
My God is my rock in
whom I find protection.
He is my shield, the strength of
my salvation, and my stronghold.

Psalm 18:2

Letter to God

Dear God,

You are a loving, responsible Father. You give us what is good for us (a carrot rather than candy). Prayer is daring when we truly seek Your will – not my will be done, but Thy will be done.

February 2002

Letter to God

Dear Lord,

As I look at the end of my life getting closer, You are taking a larger place in my life. I am only sorry I did not give You more reign in my past. But You can turn anything for Your good and I see You doing that with the days You will give me. Thank You.

Your Daughter,
Nancy

March 2002

However, I consider my life worth nothing to me, if only I may finish the race and complete the task the Lord Jesus has given me.

Acts 20:24 NIV

Letter to God

God,

Help me to finish the race…

April 2002

EPILOGUE

"BREAKING THE TAPE"

It was Sunday evening, April 29, when I realized Mom was going to leave us. Although we had been praying for miracles and we were receiving what we thought were daily victories, Mom peacefully knew that she was going home to be with the Lord. Upon her request, we turned her bed to the window, so she could enjoy a beautiful sunset over her beloved ocean. She asked about all the wonderful birds flying along the horizon. By the looks on our faces, she quickly realized that these were sacred images for her personal enjoyment. At that point, the spiritual symbol of the dove became the theme for the remainder of her life.

The next morning, my mother's friends from her long-standing church and covenant groups began appearing throughout the day. In my "prior life," I had considered many of these women to be rather strange ("natural man does not accept the things of the Spirit of God, for they are foolishness to him"), but I now understand, cherish and love every one of them. I watched as they prayed, sang and held hands – I witnessed a spiritual outpouring like never before.

Late that morning, we tracked down Aunt Judy, Mom's sister, who teaches high school in a small, central Oregon town. Mom really wanted to see her, and there was some urgency in Mom's failing voice. When we told her it would take Judy at least 10 hours to get there, some of Mom's last words were, "I'll hold on until then."

Judy drove the fours hours to Boise, caught a plane to Salt Lake City, and then made the last flight into Orange County about 10:30 p.m. Bob and I stayed at the hospital, cheering Mom on as we watched her oxygen level and pulse rate drop. We sang and encouraged her on to the "finish line." A couple of friends picked Judy up at the airport and whisked her to the hospital a little after 11 p.m. Judy spent 15 or 20 minutes alone with Mom – it was a wonderful scene.

A number of us then joined in Mom's room and fellowshipped together. We cried, we prayed, we sang joyful songs. At about 12:30 a.m., one of Mom's girlfriends whispered to me, "It's OK now, everything's OK, your mom's ready to let her spirit go, but she needs to hear it from you." I went to the head of my mother's bed, held her hand, and leaned close. I had the opportunity to say everything a son wishes he could tell his mom – every final "I love you", every last "thank you". Then I softly whispered, "Everything here is done. It's OK to let your spirit go now."

Within seconds, she peacefully started to slow down her breathing — 5 seconds between breaths, 10 seconds between breaths, 20 seconds, 30 seconds… And then, with a slight smile on her face, she drifted away and entered the loving arms of Jesus. He was so merciful, He was so faithful – there was no pain, only peace. We grieved, but we also embraced the joy of Mom entering into eternity with our Lord. At the moment her spirit departed, we could almost hear Jesus say, "Well done thy good and faithful servant."

What a precious and glorious memory for all of us. You couldn't have been in that hospital room and not left a believer...

A believer in the presence, power, love and grace of our Lord and Savior, Jesus Christ.

Thank you for sharing in Mom's heart. If I can provide any encouragement in your journey with God, please contact me at: www.WrittenHeart.com.

In Christ's Enduring Love,

Randall Niles

Writing My Heart to GOD…

As Nancy shows us, we should all seek quiet times with God. In solitude, we can explore the blessing of writing our hearts to Him. Writing is a form of worship. We don't have to be professional writers, or even good writers – it's all about the passion for God in our hearts. Journals and letters are powerful tools for recording thoughts, prayers, fears and miracles in our lives. Writing our hearts to God is a life-changing compliment to our daily devotionals with Him...

Listen...

Find a quite place and explore the power of meditative prayer and writing in your life. Learn to seek God's face during your alone times with Him. Through writing, learn to hear God's whispers in your life...

Reflect...

Who are you?

What is your background?

What experiences brought you to this time and place in your life?

Release...

What life changing mistakes have you made?

Are there any buried mistakes in your life that still hold you back?

Have you released your mistakes to God, so you can experience His true blessings for your life?

Surrender...

What event or series of events in your life brought you to your knees?

Where did you focus your thoughts and efforts during crisis?

When did you turn it all over to God?

Praise...

What victories have you experienced in your life?

What blessings has God brought your way?

Think about God's role in your life,
and give Him thanks for all you have.

Other Books in the "Writing My Heart to God" Series by Nancy Tuttle and Randall Niles:

The Prodigal Prayer

The Story of a Prayerful Mother and Prodigal Son

One of the most heart-wrenching experiences for a Christian parent is to witness a child's rebellion against Christ. This book provides encouragement to those who are feeling helpless, as they watch someone they love drift away from God. It also demonstrates the power of fervent prayer, as well as the need to be patient and persevering with our children and grandchildren. It's about viewing the "prodigal experience" as a spiritual process, which helps build and strengthen our faith in God's plan for our loved ones.

Purpose in Trial

Finding Joy & Meaning in the Midst of Cancer

Here is the story of how one woman found peace and joy in the midst of cancer. Nancy spent the last seven years of her life battling this disease, but saw the eternal purposes for it, beyond the temporal pain. In the midst of her suffering, she found new meaning and a depth to God's love. Her hope is that what she has discovered will help you cope with the trials in your life, reach out to someone going through cancer, or maybe even change your life altogether.

To Order Copies of "Correspondence with God" or other Titles by Nancy Tuttle:

1. **Call 949-951-8969;**
2. **Order online: www.KenosisPublishing.com; or**
3. **Fill out this Form and Fax (949-420-0276) or Mail to:**
Kenosis Publishing, LLC.
20532 El Toro Rd. Suite 209
Mission Viejo, CA 92692

Name ______________________________

Address ______________________________

Address ______________________________

City ________________ State _____ Zip _____

Credit Card Number: ________________ Exp. Date: _____

Alternate payment method (circle one) check money order

E-mail address: ______________________________

Phone: ____________________

Quantity:

________ The Prodigal Prayer

________ Correspondence With God

________ Purpose in Trial

Quantity of Books: _____ X $6.99 ea. $ ____________

Shipping* $ ____________

Tax** $ ____________

Shipment Total $ ____________

* ***Shipping:*** *(1) Book $1.50 Additional Books: $.35 each*

** ***Taxes:*** *California residents, add 7.75% sales tax.*

Note: We only accept Visa or Mastercard if paying by credit card.

(Call for discounts on bulk orders for churches, ministries and resellers.)